Follow us on Facebook @creativechameleonbooks
creativechameleonbooks@gmail.com

Also by Creative Chameleon Books
Anxious Armadillo
Gorgeous George
Cranky Crab
Theodore James Harrison Brown
I'm Better Than You!

Text copyright © 2021 by Karen Lord
Illustrations copyright © 2021 by Shanée Buxton
First published in 2021

All rights reserved.
No part of this book may be reproduced in any form or by any means, electronic or mechanical, including photocopying, recording or by any information storage and retrieval system, without the prior written permission of the authors.

Being kind is powerful!

Rayan

Be thoughtful.

Karen and Shanée

Her wings glistened in the sun, reflecting in the pond,
As she stared into the distance, she heard a sound beyond.

Tzz

Tzz

Tzz

Tzz Tzz Tzz Tzz

In they flew, boisterous and bold,
Raucous, rowdy, wicked and cold.
Their eyes as dark as a thunder cloud,
Mosquitoes lairy,
             Mosquitoes loud.

Mosquitoes mean, malicious and menacing,
Dark, daring, terrifying and threatening.
With featherlike hairs across their backs,
Vile, destructive, ready to attack.

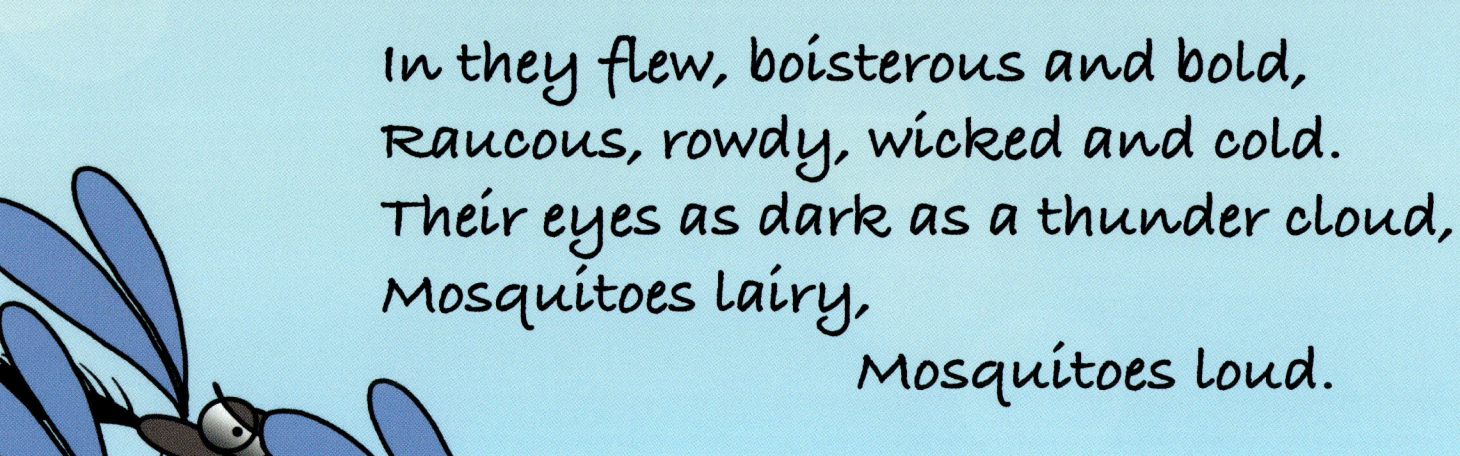

They circled the dragonfly, taunting, teasing,
"Oh, look at her! How displeasing!
With her delicate wings and eyes shining bright,
So quiet and timid, let's give her a fright!"

"Hey, dragonfly! Oh, dragonfly! Why do you quake,
With your transparent wings that shimmer and shake?"

"Budge off that lily leaf, you can't stay and chat.
This pond is ours, so scoot! GET LOST! SCAT!"

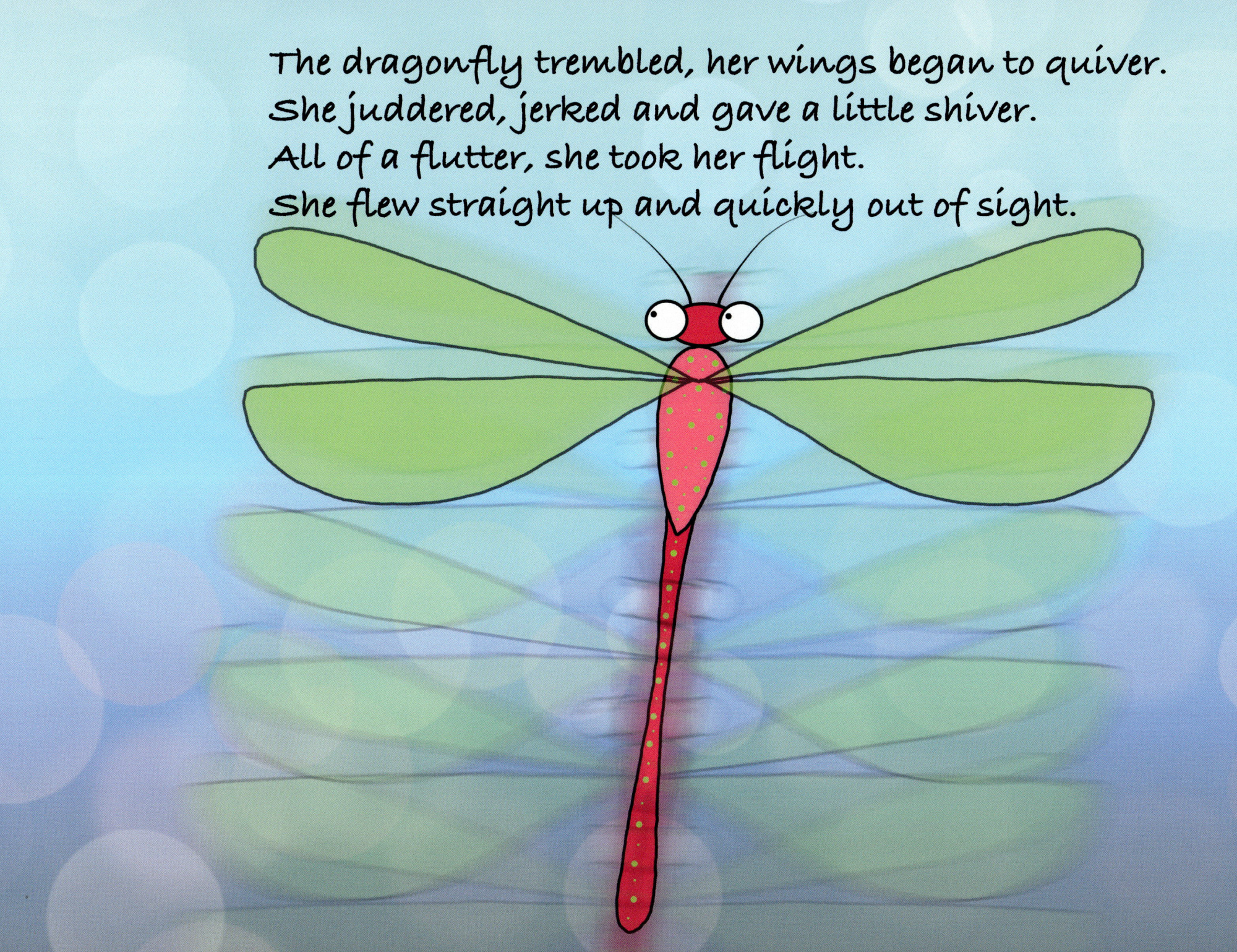

The dragonfly trembled, her wings began to quiver.
She juddered, jerked and gave a little shiver.
All of a flutter, she took her flight.
She flew straight up and quickly out of sight.

Her wings sparkled in the sunlight, casting rainbows in the lake,
When across the shimmering water, came sounds you could not mistake.

Tzz

Tzz

Tzz

Tzz Tzz Tzz Tzz

In they flew, boisterous and bold,
Raucous, rowdy, wicked and cold.
Their eyes as dark as a thunder cloud,
Mosquitoes lairy,
                Mosquitoes loud.

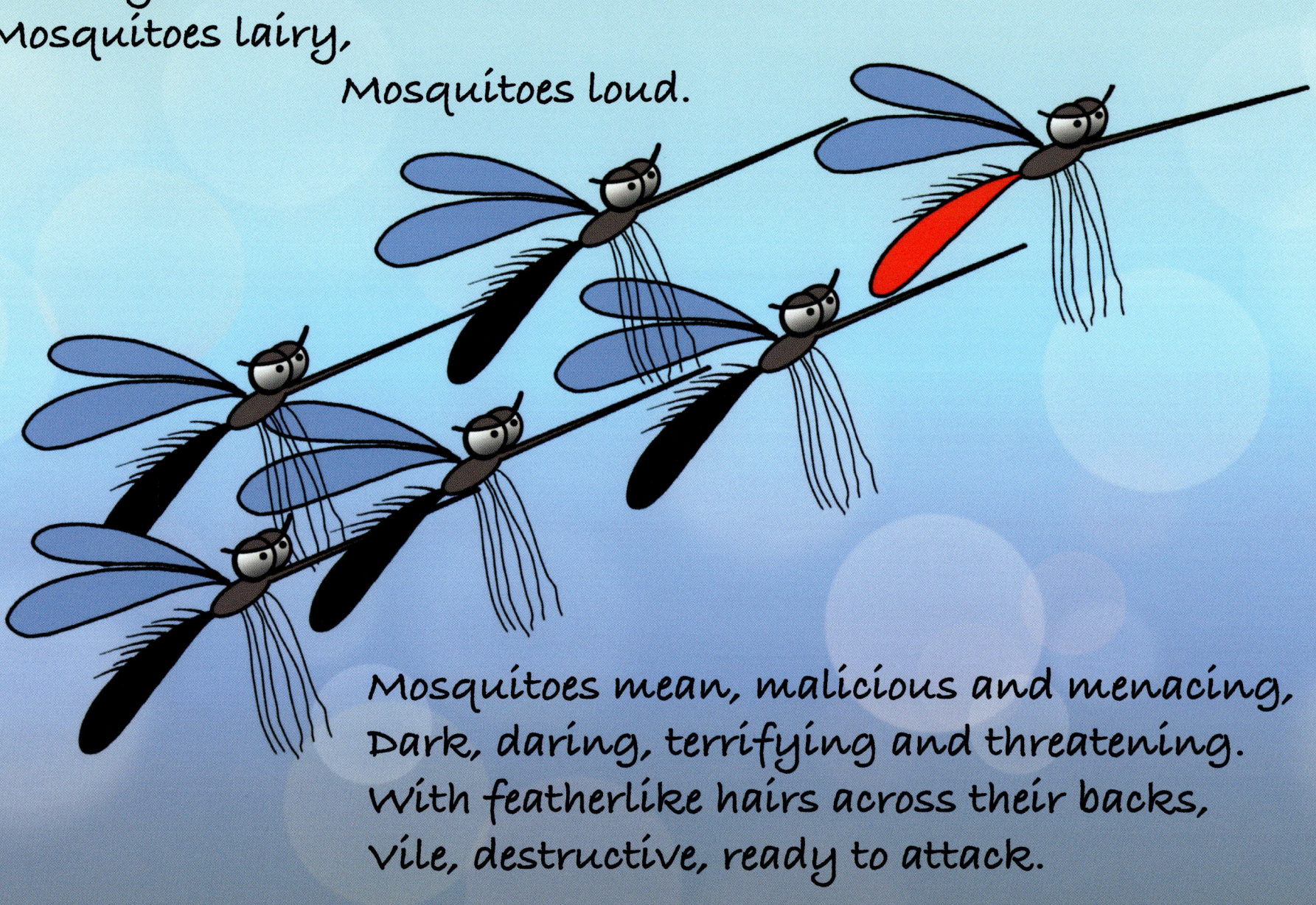

Mosquitoes mean, malicious and menacing,
Dark, daring, terrifying and threatening.
With featherlike hairs across their backs,
Vile, destructive, ready to attack.

They swooped down to the dragonfly, pestering, provoking,
"Oh, look at her! She must be joking!
With her delicate wings and eyes shining bright,
So quiet and timid, let's give her a fright!"

"Hey, dragonfy! Oh, dragonfly! Fancy seeing you, we're charmed!
We must stop meeting like this, now don't look so alarmed."

"Get out of the pickerel weed, it belongs to us!
This lake is out of bounds. Now leave without a fuss!"

The dragonfly trembled, her wings began to quiver.
She juddered, jerked and gave a little shiver.
All of a flutter, she took her flight.
She flew straight up and quickly out of sight.

Her wings moved quickly up and down, the reeds lightly danced,
As closer and closer, the mosquito army advanced.

In they flew, boisterous and bold,
Raucous, rowdy, wicked and cold.
Their eyes as dark as a thunder cloud,
Mosquitoes lairy,
                Mosquitoes loud.

Mosquitoes mean, malicious and menacing,
Dark, daring, terrifying and threatening.
With featherlike hairs across their backs,
Vile, destructive, ready to attack.

The marsh reeds parted from every direction.
Mosquitoes flew in, with anger and aggression.
They descended like arrows, shot out of a bow,
Scoffing and sneering, she had nowhere to go!

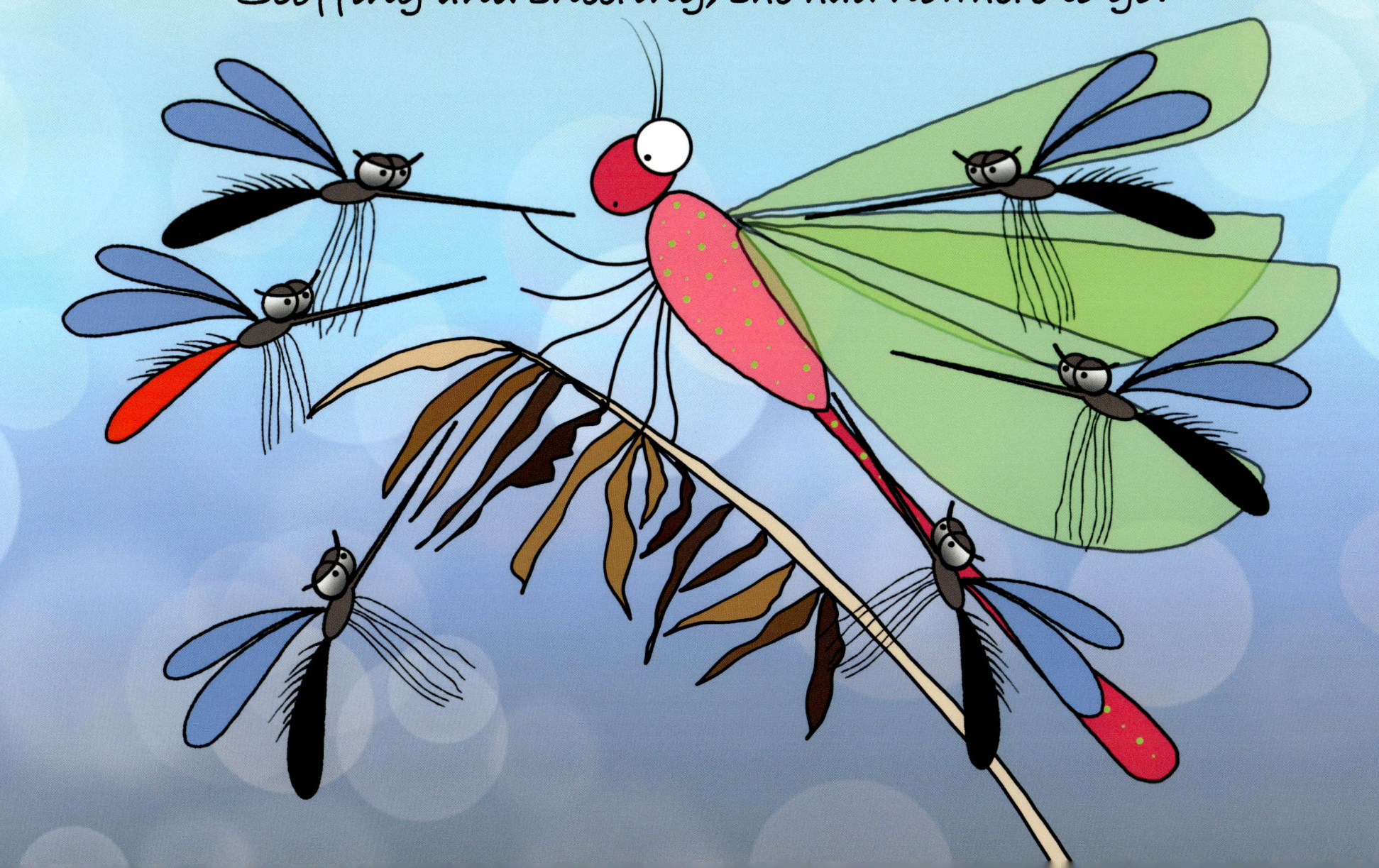

"Hey, dragonfy! Oh, dragonfly! So, what brings you here,
With your pretty face, oh, dragonfly dear?
The marshland is ours!" the mosquitoes yelled with a roar,
"And we have told you this, so many times before!"

They knocked dragonfly off the tall marsh reed,
And taunted, jeered, poked and teased.
Her wings shivered and with a very big thud,
The mosquitoes pushed her down in the sticky brown mud.

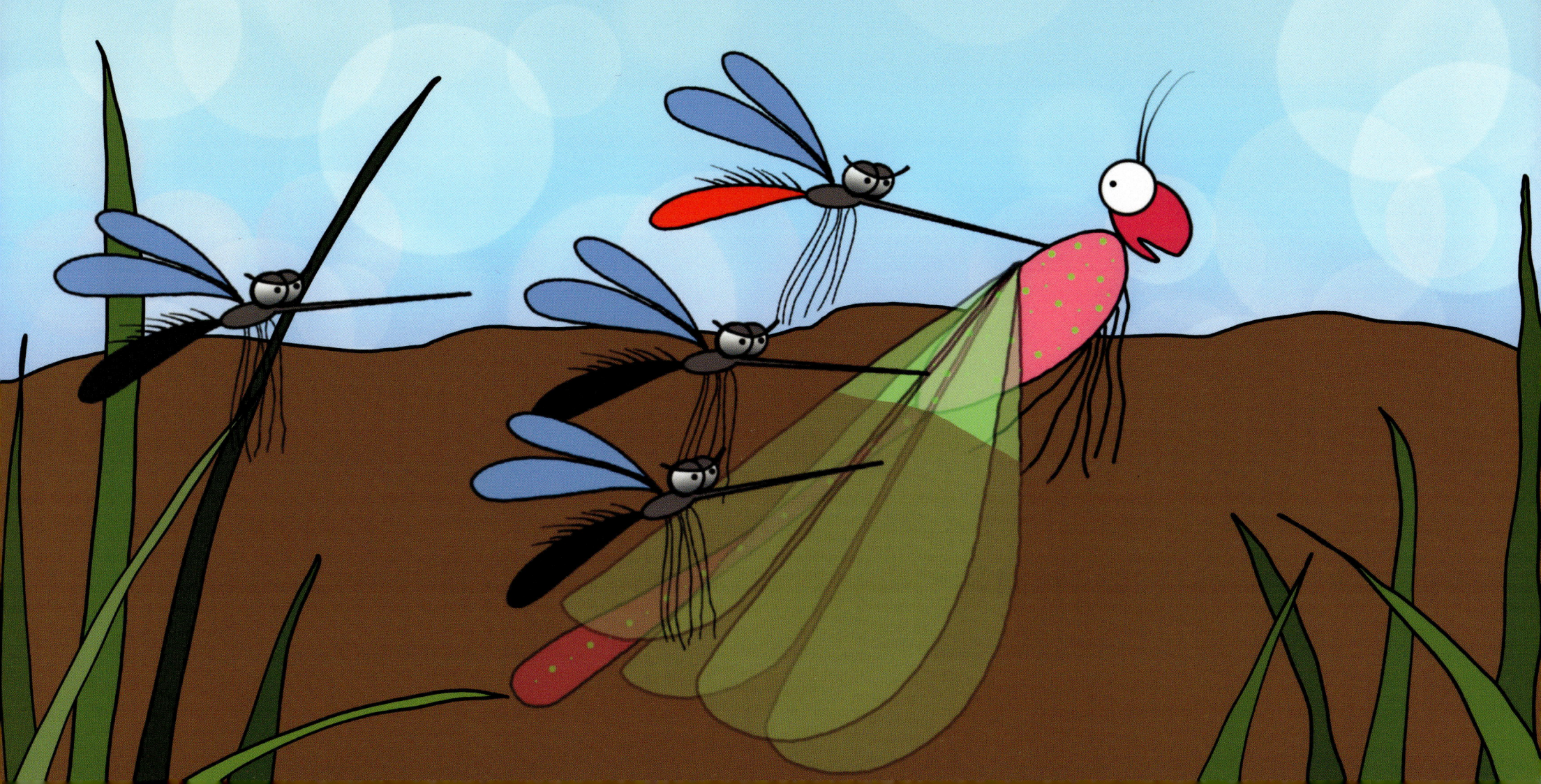

"Not so beautiful now!" a young mosquito laughed,
"How did you enjoy your cooling mud bath?
You do not belong here, there is no room for you,
If we catch you again, who knows what we'll do!"

They circled around her and wickedly sneered,
"You think you are pretty, you're not, you're just WEIRD!
Now fly away, dragonfly, find another place to rest,
With your dirty wings and mud stained chest!"

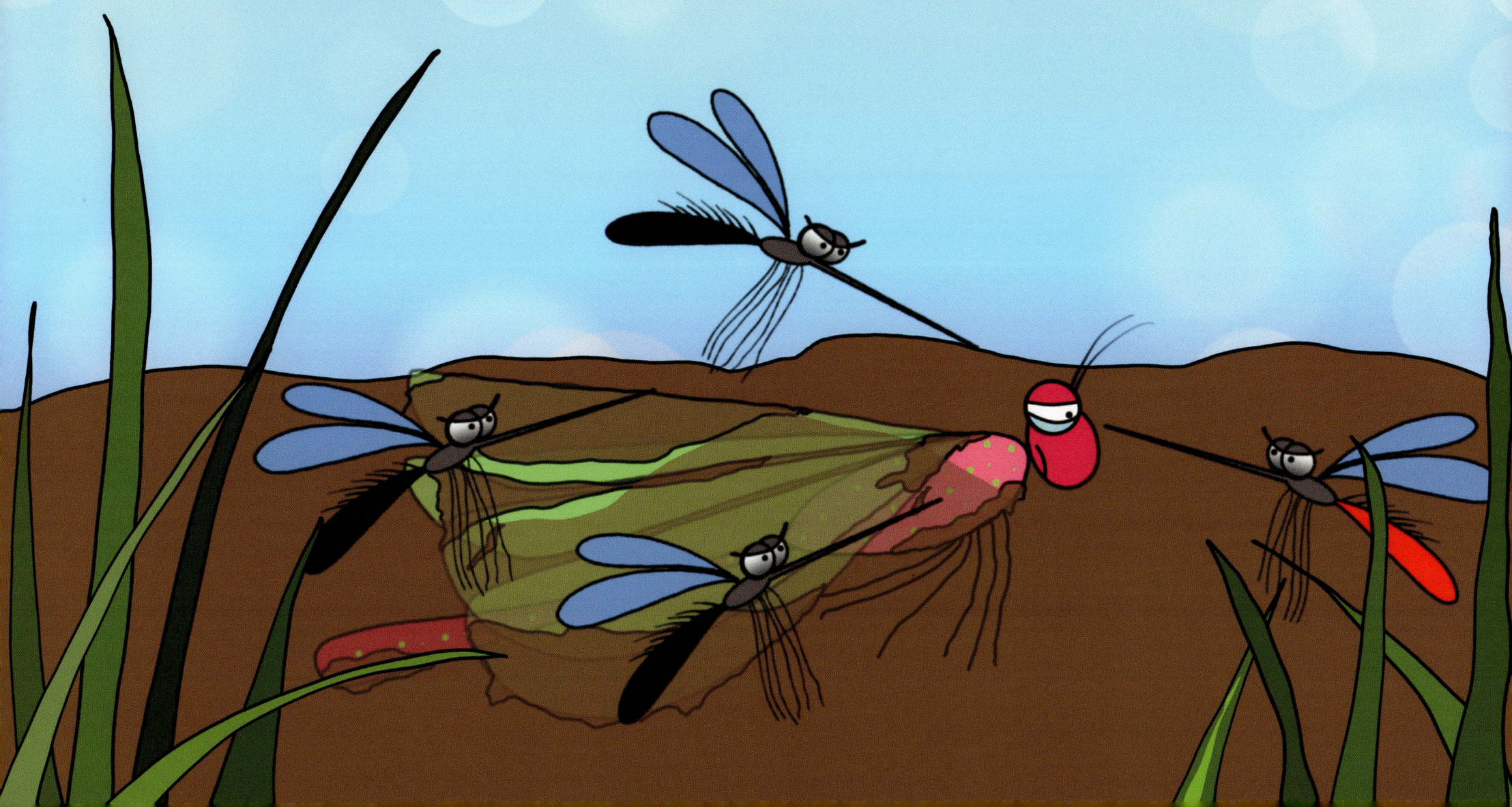

Dark evil eyes looked down on dragonfly,
Whose muddy face lifted with a whimper and a cry.
Her nose slowly twitched, with the scent of the morning,
When an unfamiliar sound was heard without warning.

The damselflies hovered above the swamp marsh.

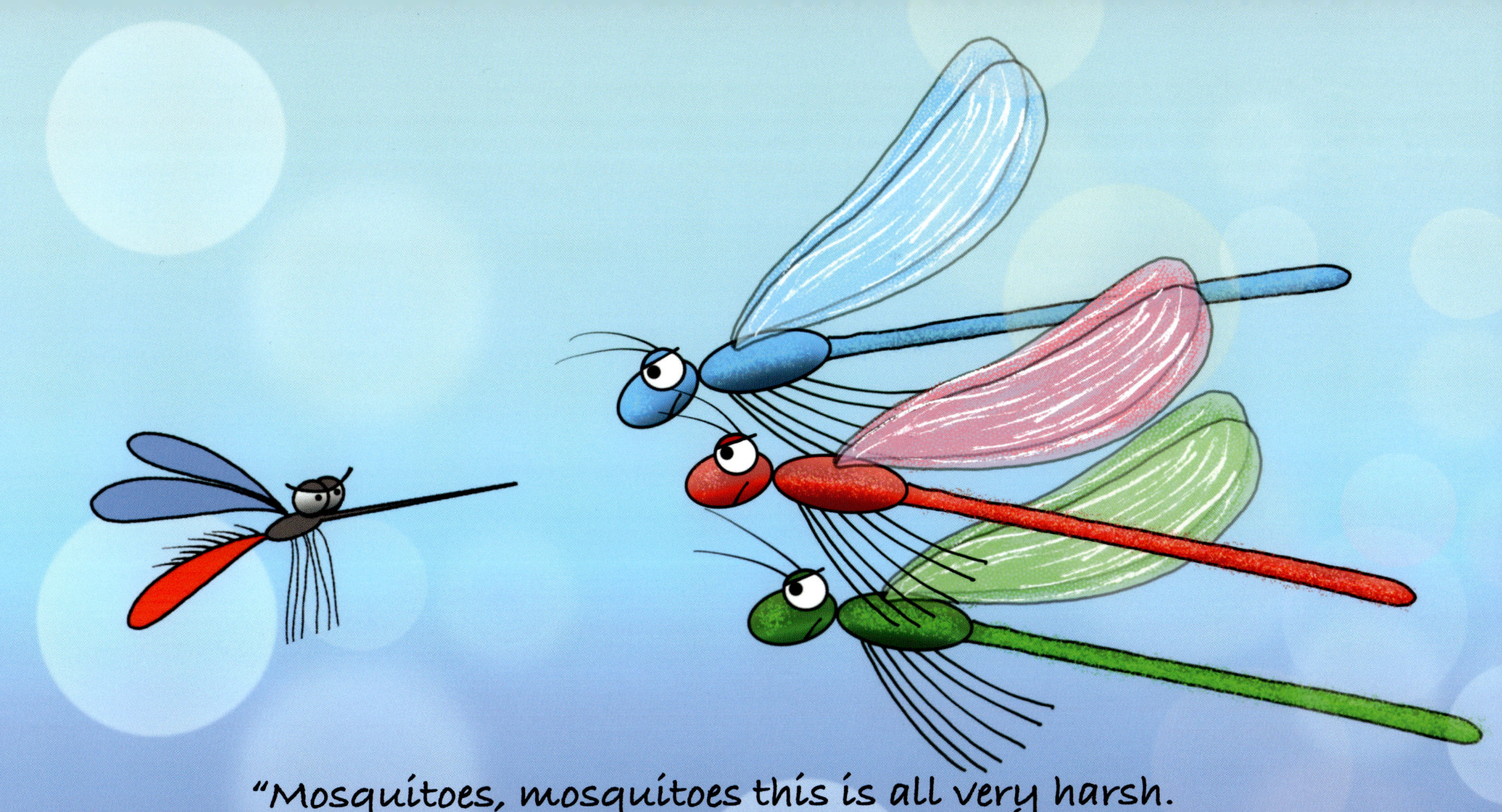

"Mosquitoes, mosquitoes this is all very harsh.
Your hassling and heckling is not wanted here,
Teasing and tormenting, putting lives in fear.
Indignant, insulting, this is the final time,
You either leave this lake or learn to tow the line!"

Dragonfly fluttered her wings and pushed herself up tall.
She stuttered to find her voice, which was tiny and small.
"I've tried to ignore you...I've tried to stay strong,
Your words have been spiteful, it's been going on too long."

You did the right thing, dragonfly," a damselfly cried,
"When you spoke to us yesterday, you were hurting inside.
You were very courageous letting us know,
How these mosquitoes have stooped so low."

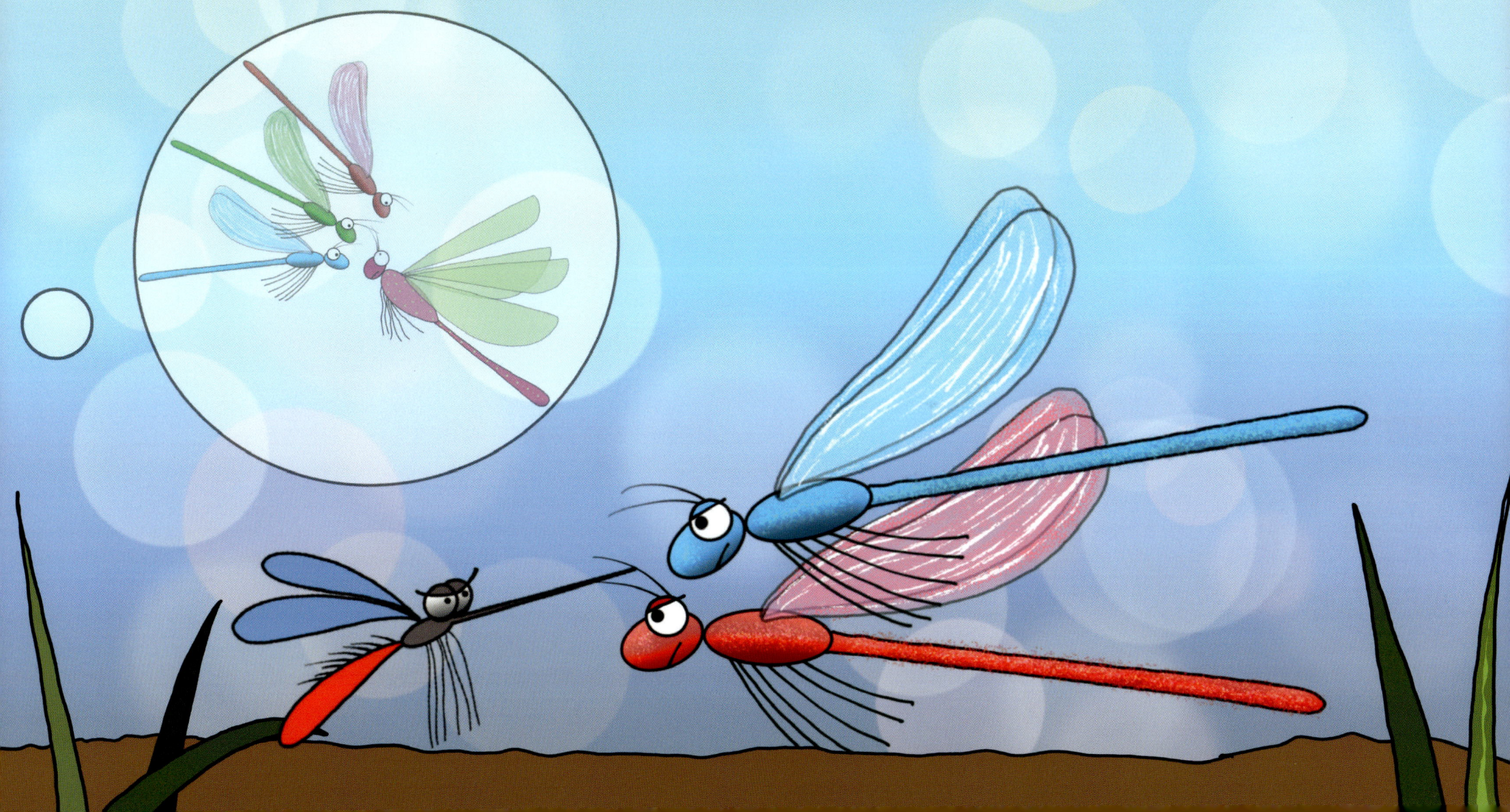

"They singled you out, when they made their attack,
And you just flew off and did not fight back.
You were frightened and scared, so it was brave of you,
To find some help, as that's not easy to do."

"Mosquitoes, mosquitoes, you think you're so tough,
But it's silly, foolish, rude and rough.
Your bullying ways do not impress us at all!
You are cowardly, weak and not very cool."

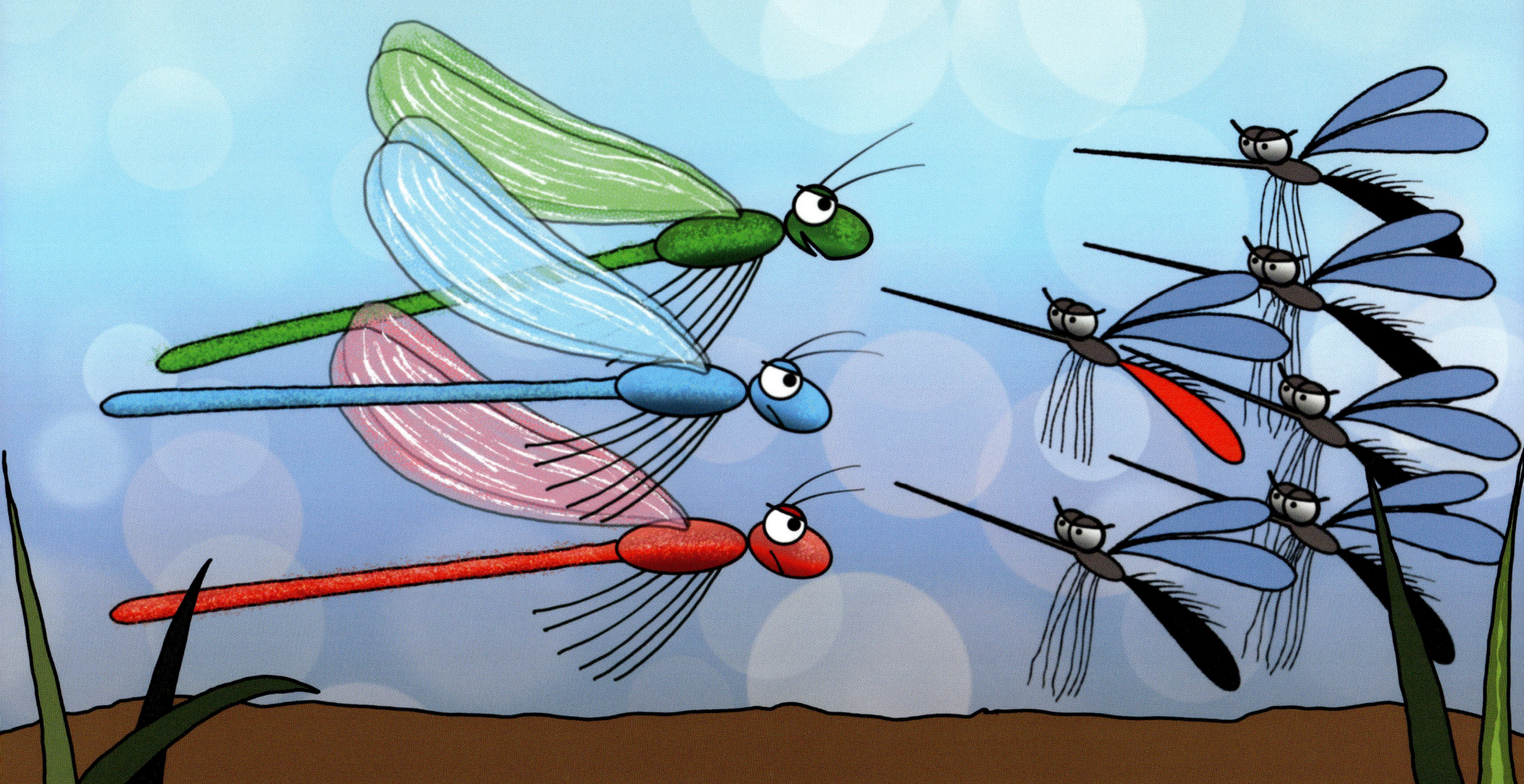

Mosquitoes silent.

Mosquitoes still.

No lairy or loud and out for the thrill.

Their dark eyes faded and hairs on their back drooped...

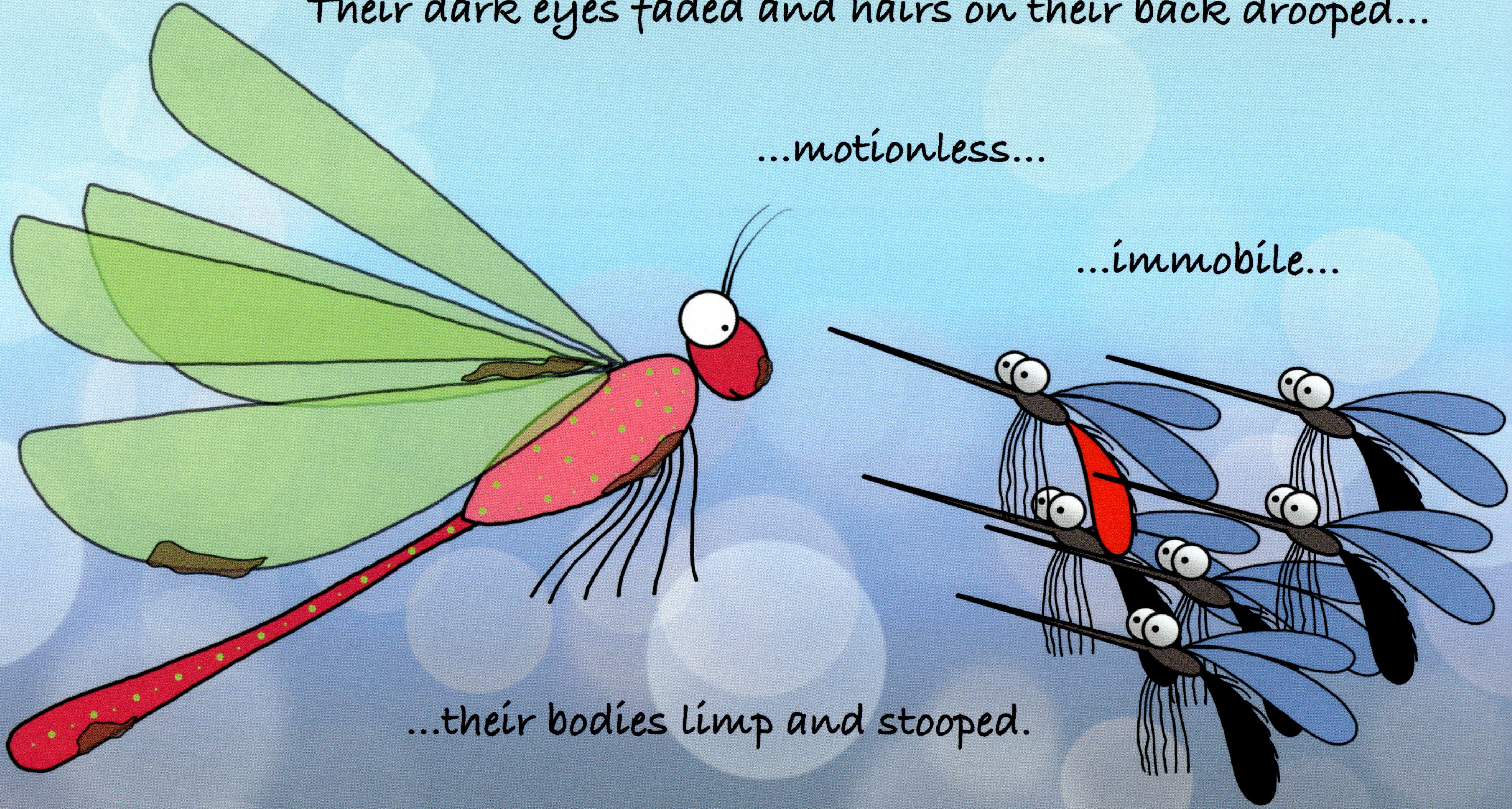

...motionless...

...immobile...

...their bodies limp and stooped.

Suddenly, their heads quickly moved from side to side.
They had been caught in the act, with nowhere to hide.
Taking one look at the dragonfy, they glanced at the ground,
And lifted their wings, flying off without sound.

...and on a Sunday, next to the water lettuce weed,

A dragonfly hovered gracefully ready to feed.

unruffled...undisturbed...

..uninterrupted...

...and with no worries in the world.